My father says that I need to eat more *always* foods and less *sometimes* foods. I think he means I should eat more fruit and vegetables.

'You are what you eat,' he always says.

I know that's not true. Today I ate three donuts but I didn't turn into one.

My mother says that I need to spend more time playing outside.

‘If you spend all day inside, you’ll turn into a mushroom,’ she always says.

I don’t think that’s true.

My brother says that I spend too much time watching TV.

'You'll end up turning into a couch potato if you're not careful,' he always says.

I don't think that's true.

My sister says that I need to laugh more.

'If the wind changes direction, you'll end up with a frown frozen on your face,' she always says.

I don't think that's true.

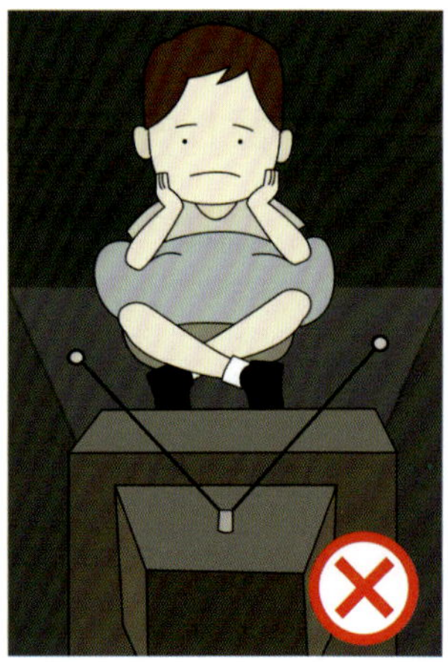

My father says that I spend too much time in front of the screen.

'You'll end up with square eyes if you're not careful,' he always says.

I don't think that's true.

My mother says that I need to exercise more.

'Your legs will fall off if you don't use them,' she always says.

I don't think that's true.

My brother tried to teach me a new trick.

'No thanks,' I said. 'It's too hard.'

'Your brain will turn into mush if you don't try to learn new things,' he said.

I don't think that's true.

My sister says that I need to get lots of sleep each night.

'Looking at a screen too much before going to bed can wake you up during the night,' she said.

'I don't think that's true,' I said, holding back a yawn.

My father says that I need to help out others more.

'It's better to give than to receive,' he always says.

I'm not sure if that's true.

My mother says that I need to spend less time glued to my devices.

'Take some time out and smell the roses,' she always says.

I'm not sure what that means and so I don't know if that's true.

My family says that I don't seem as happy as I used to be. They say that my friends don't come around to play anymore.

I think that is true.

My friends say that they are worried about me.

'We miss the old you,' they said.

I'm not sure what to think about that. Maybe it's true – I have been feeling a bit down lately. I better talk to Mum and Dad.

'Healthy mind, healthy body,' said my mother.

'You know all about healthy choices,' said my father. 'Only you can decide if you want to make changes and choose those healthy choices. It's called changing your *mindset.'*

That sounds like it's true.

‘I wish I could change,’ I said to my family.

‘Wishing doesn’t work,’ said my father. ‘You have to act and take the first step. The first step is the hardest.’

I know that’s true.

'Let's go outside and have a water pistol fight,' I said to my family.

'Great idea,' said my sister.

'Parents verse kids,' said my brother.

'But Mum and Dad always win,' said my father.

I know that's not true.

My father says my mindset is changing.

'It hasn't been easy,' I said.

'Changing old habits never is,' said my mother.

That is so true.

Activities

Look at the images on this page. Talk about what other activities you can do outside during the day.

Look at the images on this page. Talk about what other activities you can do during the day while inside.

Look at the images on this page. Talk about what other activities you can do during the day at home.

Look at the images on this page. Talk about what other activities you can do at night.

Knowledge Books and Software
Reproduction and Communication for educational purposes
Reproduction and Communication for other purposes
POBox 50, Sandgate, Queensland 4017 Australia
p. +617-5568 0288 f. +617-5568 0277 email: sales@kbs.com.au

First published 2016

ISBN 9781925398274

Author: Michael Paulsen
Illustrator: Ed Crisostomo
Layup and design: Dean Maynard
Producer: Corey White
Publisher: Rob Watts

Series information: Healthy Me! series

CHANGING YOUR MINDSET

My family is worried about me. They say I am not making healthy choices. I'm not sure I agree with them. Then again, sometimes I think they might be right. I would like to make some changes but it all seems too hard.

ISBN 9781925398274

10 Healthy Me